SPORTS BIOGRAPHIES

TOM BRADY

KENNY ABDO

Fly!
An Imprint of Abdo Zoom
abdobooks.com

abdobooks.com

Published by Abdo Zoom, a division of ABDO, P.O. Box 398166, Minneapolis,
Minnesota 55439. Copyright © 2022 by Abdo Consulting Group, Inc. International
copyrights reserved in all countries. No part of this book may be reproduced in any
form without written permission from the publisher. Fly!™ is a trademark and logo
of Abdo Zoom.

Printed in the United States of America, North Mankato, Minnesota.
052021
092021

THIS BOOK CONTAINS
RECYCLED MATERIALS

Photo Credits: Alamy, AP Images, Icon Sportswire, iStock,
Seth Poppel/Yearbook Library, Shutterstock, ©BrokenSphere p8 /CC BY-SA 3.0
Production Contributors: Kenny Abdo, Jennie Forsberg, Grace Hansen
Design Contributors: Dorothy Toth, Neil Klinepier

Library of Congress Control Number: 2021933240

Publisher's Cataloging-in-Publication Data

Names: Abdo, Kenny, author
Title: Tom Brady / by Kenny Abdo
Description: Minneapolis, Minnesota : Abdo Publishing, 2022 | Series: Sports
    Biographies | Includes online resources and index
Identifiers: ISBN 9781098226527 (lib. bdg.) | ISBN 9781098226541 (ebook) |
    ISBN 9781098226558 (Read-to-Me ebook)
Subjects: LCSH: Brady, Tom, 1977---Juvenile literature. | Quarterbacks (Football)-
    United States--Biography--Juvenile literature. | Tampa Bay Buccaneers (Football
    team)--Juvenile literature. | Professional athletes--United States--Biography-
    Juvenile literature. | Super Bowl--Records--Juvenile literature.
Classification: DDC 796.332092--dc23

TABLE OF CONTENTS

TOM BRADY

Many believe Tom Brady is the greatest quarterback of all time. With countless wins and records, he has proven the believers to be right.

Brady has racked up 10 **Super Bowl** appearances, seven rings, and 13 other Big Game records in his 20-plus-year career at quarterback (QB).

EARLY YEARS

Thomas Brady Jr. was born in
San Mateo, California, in 1977.

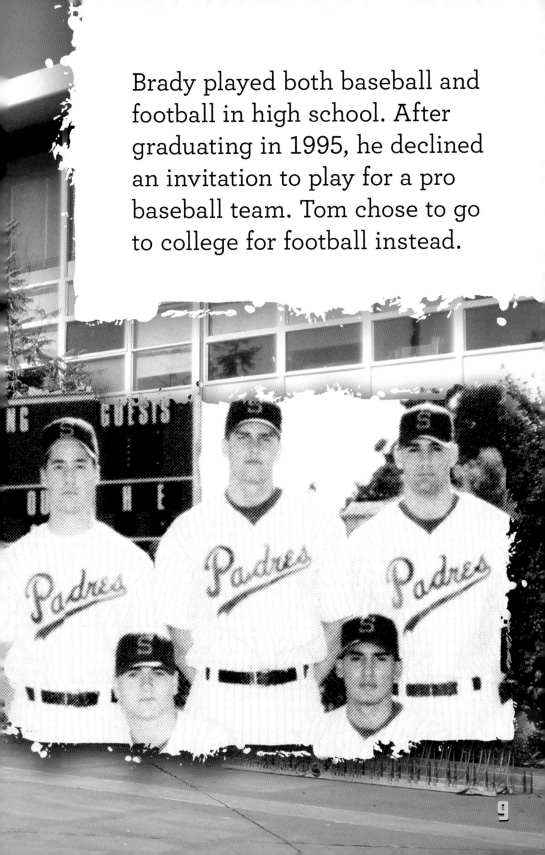

Brady played both baseball and football in high school. After graduating in 1995, he declined an invitation to play for a pro baseball team. Tom chose to go to college for football instead.

Brady played quarterback for the University of Michigan. The Wolverines won the **Orange Bowl** in his final season.

GOING PRO

In 2000, Brady was **drafted** by the New England Patriots. He started his career as the **fourth-string** QB. By season's end, he had worked his way up the roster to second in line.

13

MILLOY

CHAMP

Patriots

SUPER BOWL
XXX

Drew Bledsoe went down early in the 2001 season with an injury. Tom stepped in. Brady won his first game at starting QB and then 10 more in the regular season. The Patriots went all the way to the **Super Bowl** and won! The 24-year-old was named Super Bowl **MVP**.

Brady led the Patriots to two more
Super Bowl wins following the 2003
and 2004 seasons. In 2005, Brady
signed a new **contract**. A few pricey
extensions followed. But Brady proved
to be worth the investment.

Brady and the Patriots won an incredible three more **Super Bowls** behind the 2014, 2016, and 2018 seasons. In 2020, after 20 years with New England, Brady moved to sunnier weather in Tampa Bay.

If any Buccaneers fan worried that Brady's greatness stayed in New England, their mind was quickly put at ease. Tampa Bay made it to the playoffs for the first time since 2007. Then they cruised all the way to **Super Bowl** LV and won it!

LEGACY

When Brady is not on the field, he works with charities. After many years with Best Buddies International, he became the global ambassador for the organization in 2019.

Brady holds an incredible number of NFL records, with others still within reach. Two teams have been lucky enough to have Brady at QB, but every team respects him for his **dedication** to the game.

GLOSSARY

contract – a legally written agreement to play for one team for a certain amount of time.

dedication – self-sacrificing devotion and loyalty.

drafted – selected to play for a team from a pool of eligible athletes.

fourth-string – belonging to the fourth string of a team. Fourth strings play behind the 1st, 2nd, and 3rd strings in that position.

MVP – short for "most valuable player," an award given in sports to a player who has performed the best in a game or series.

Orange Bowl – a yearly American college football game played in Miami since 1935.

Super Bowl – the annual NFL championship game.

ONLINE RESOURCES

Booklinks
NONFICTION NETWORK
FREE! ONLINE NONFICTION RESOURCES

To learn more about
Tom Brady, please visit
abdobooklinks.com or scan
this QR code. These links
are routinely monitored
and updated to provide the
most current information
available.

INDEX